MOONBEAMS
AND
MELTED SPOONS

MOONBEAMS AND MELTED SPOONS

A COLLECTION OF POETRY

LISSI SENEWAY

Copyright © 2022 Lissi Seneway.

All rights reserved. No part of this book may be used or reproduced by any means, graphic, electronic, or mechanical, including photocopying, recording, taping or by any information storage retrieval system without the written permission of the author except in the case of brief quotations embodied in critical articles and reviews.

This is a work of fiction. All of the characters, names, incidents, organizations, and dialogue in this novel are either the products of the author's imagination or are used fictitiously.

Archway Publishing books may be ordered through booksellers or by contacting:

Archway Publishing
1663 Liberty Drive
Bloomington, IN 47403
www.archwaypublishing.com
844-669-3957

Because of the dynamic nature of the Internet, any web addresses or links contained in this book may have changed since publication and may no longer be valid. The views expressed in this work are solely those of the author and do not necessarily reflect the views of the publisher, and the publisher hereby disclaims any responsibility for them.

Any people depicted in stock imagery provided by Getty Images are models, and such images are being used for illustrative purposes only. Certain stock imagery © Getty Images.

Interior Image Credit: Coral Condy

ISBN: 978-1-6657-2698-6 (sc)
ISBN: 978-1-6657-2696-2 (hc)
ISBN: 978-1-6657-2697-9 (e)

Library of Congress Control Number: 2022913170

Print information available on the last page.

Archway Publishing rev. date: 11/11/2022

This book is dedicated to my Aunt Ag,
my partner in crazy minds.
I love you.
Thank you for the powerful legacy you left us all.

ACKNOWLEDGMENTS

Thank you, Jonas, for your unconditional support, guidance, and love. You have helped me become the woman I am.

Thank you, Elizabeth, my kindred spirit, for pouring over this manuscript with me. Your friendship means the world. I love you, sis.

FOREWORD

I became collegially acquainted with Lissi Seneway 15 years ago. We have had the opportunity to work together and are now dear friends.

There are people who may look at clinicians as heroes. However, very few people see the times of defeat. Very few people see the exhaustion, the long hours, the emotional strain. It takes deep empathy and dedication to devote yourself to working in the trenches of therapy. Mental illness, substance abuse, and trauma are an everyday reality. Like Lissi, I know the toll this career takes, though the feeling of gratitude when we see a client overcome their obstacles is amazing.

Lissi is one of the most diligent, caring, and skilled therapists I know. Through her years of experience, she has met people from all walks of life – veterans, trauma survivors, drug addicts and their families, and former criminals. You may not be able to directly relate to the stories you are about to read, but each poem is written in such a way that you get a bird's-eye view into the characters' minds and hearts.

When Lissi asked me to write the foreword to *Moonbeams and Melted Spoons* due to my background in writing, I gave a lot of thought as to how to describe her work. If you combine the writing style of Jack Kerouac, the brutal, emotional honesty of Sylvia Plath, and the guttural literary poignancy of Jim Carroll, you have Lissi's poetry. Her writing is raw, honest, painful, and beautiful. Lissi invites you on this tour as a guide to her stories but warns you to keep your hands in the boat.

You may relate to Lissi's poems or be glad that you are enjoying them in the comfort of your home, thankful that you never had to experience the content. Whatever it is, you can't ignore it. It's like a knife in your soul, but you beg for more. Enjoy reading!

~Adam Freilich, BA, CAP, IC/RC-ADC

PREFACE

"There is no coming to consciousness without pain." - Carl Jung

I penned my first poem at age 12. Creative writing has always been a part of my life. My childhood brought trying times and writing poetry and short stories started as an escape. It allowed me to release heavy emotions I did not quite understand. Writing has evolved into my passion; creativity is a channel for my spirituality, my work, and sometimes my own trials and tribulations.

As a life-long student of psychology, I have learned that all human beings experience the entire spectrum of emotion, including joy, ecstasy, happiness, grief, sorrow, rage, confusion, fear, and even hate. The negative emotions are inescapable but acknowledging our darker side can help us find life in the light. Many eastern and western philosophies and religions recognize there is darkness and light in the universe and in human beings – angels and demons, the yin and yang, the true self and the ego.

Throughout my career as a psychotherapist, I have born witness to gaping emotional wounds and layers of pain. I have forged battlefields of mental wars with people who fight the brutalist, ugliest, and scariest parts of themselves. I have heard countless deeply personal life stories. It is an honor to be in the presence of such vulnerability. I try to help people fight their demons and win back their lives.

The pieces in this collection are written from unique perspectives. The protagonists include veterans, survivors of sexual assault and child abuse, alcoholics and drug addicts, and people struggling with mental health disorders. The poems do not necessarily have proverbial "happy endings," but in real life, many people with these types of experiences do find peace.

My hope is that you enjoy reading these poems. You may even connect with one of the characters. Perhaps you have stepped away from a relationship, have been touched by substance abuse or mental illness, carry pain from childhood, or have inner turmoil. As social creatures, we must be able to identify and connect with other humans. Oftentimes, we feel we are the only ones who are carrying a particular pain. When we identify with someone else's story, suddenly we do not feel so alone.

I want to give a voice to those who have not found theirs yet. I also hope to spread awareness of issues that are exceedingly difficult to handle and comprehend. The topics in my poetry can be frightening and are quite misunderstood. Reading from the various protagonists' perspective may help you gain insight into and an understanding of these debilitating battles.

If you are having a tough time emotionally, mentally, or spiritually, I strongly encourage you to talk to a mentor, clergy, or a professional. Remember, identifying the darkness can show you to a life of light. As Viktor Frankel said, "What is to give light must endure burning."

CONTENTS

Book I: Fractals and Chaos

Infinite	1
Red Wine and Moonbeams	2
'O Sweet Child	4
Window Shopping	5
Lost Fall	10
Have Some Cake	12
Animal Kingdom	15
How Does Your Garden Grow?	17
Do͟n͟'͟t͟ ͟f͟o͟rget the Water	19

Book II: Keeping Up with the Joneses

I Declare War	23
plastered disaster	24
The List	27
Stardust	29
Red Wagon	31
An Ode to Stargazers	34
tic toc	36

Cat and Mouse	40
The Wheel	43
Shoot to Kill	46
Blue	49

Book III: Alien-ation

Extraterrestrial Beings and Such	53
The King's Table	54
The Eyewall	57
Mourning Dove	62
Bloodletting	65
Sold	67
Moving Picture	70

Book IV: Toxicology

A Virulent Strain	75
The Land of Nod	76
Invocation	79
Emma	81
Dance, Ballerina, Dance	83
Detonated Heart	86
Pray for Rain	88

Vanishing Act	90
Red Leaves in Manhattan	92
Endless Lives	94

Book V: Casualties of Eve

une femme triste	99
Melissa	100
Girl Gone Mad	103
Daddies and Daughters	106
Fearless	110
A Letter from Sylvia	113
Body Betrayed	115
My Name is Lisette!	118
Pretty	121
Did you know?	123
A Declination of Grace	126

Book VI: The Unfortunate Sons of Cain

Wrath	131
Man Alone	132
His Lovers	134
David and Goliath	136

Muse	139
A Penitent	141
20 to Life	143
Animation Fascination	148
Great Scott	151
Home for the Holidays	153
Epilogue	157

BOOK I
FRACTALS AND CHAOS

INFINITE

Shocking circles repeating

Repeating

Repeating

Butterfly wings flapping

Flapping

Flapping

I am not predictable

Do not test me

You'll lose yourself

In my

Turbulence

RED WINE AND MOONBEAMS

I hear her sing, words slurred.

She is such a mystery. The legacy of pain, strange and insane. Unexplained.

Memories flood. I feel the heat in my blood.

Her voice echoes in my brain,

"I remember the day you came."

Her wave is imprinted.

Red wine and moonbeams.

I'm a rock star with shattered dreams.

Realizations, resignations. Searched so high, searched so low, to piece together my history.

On the sand of my mind space, I hear the broken songbird sounds, inhale the pungent smells, envision piercing blue.

Who were you?

The last time I saw her, the final goodbye. But I didn't cry!

Red wine and moonbeams.

I'm a rock star with shattered dreams.

Realizations, resignations. Searched so high, searched so low, just to know why I'll never know my history.

Tears stream as the sun gleams. I have no fight as I drift off to sleep.

Red wine and moonbeams.

          I'm a rock star.

                    I'm a shattered dream.

'O SWEET CHILD

Hush, little baby,
> don't say a word,
even though Daddy never
> bought you a mockingbird.
Who needs a mockingbird, anyway?
> Wipe away those tears, you'll be okay.
Just hush, little baby,
> 'cuz Daddy's not really dead.
But the devil came to him
> and fucked with his head.
As you lay your little self down to sleep,
> pray to the Lord your soul to keep,
to save you from the demons
> that stole Daddy away in the night.
Please hush, little baby,
> don't you cry.
I'm sure your Daddy's sorry
> for not saying goodbye.

WINDOW SHOPPING

Strolling down the city sidewalks,

the snow falls in the most charming patterns.

I try to catch flakes on my tongue.

*

I put my arm through my lover's arm. We laugh and kiss and move closer.

He says something witty - I giggle and marvel over his intelligence as we pass a Christmas display behind a frosty window.

*

I point to the figurines gathered around the aluminum Christmas tree, plastic smiles on their faces, with forever rosy cheeks.

I say, "Darling, that will be you and I and our children someday, gathered around our own tree, surrounded by colorfully wrapped gifts."

He kisses the tip of my nose and tells me my eyes are sparkling like the North Star.

I sigh and rest my head on his shoulder as we discuss our wonderful life and plan our first holiday together.

*

Right in the middle of my description of our Christmas dinner

(I plan on cooking a huge ham, you see, a ham so grand you wouldn't believe how good it will taste)

a passerby stops and looks at me in an odd sort of way. This man, dressed in a three-piece suit and a long, gray overcoat asks, "Excuse me, miss, but whom are you speaking with?"

*

I press my face so close to the frosty window I can see my own breath forming a small circle on the glass.

I say to this man in his three-piece suit, "Sir, as you can see, we are window shopping and planning our Christmas dinner.

I'm cooking a ham so grand you wouldn't believe how good it will taste. I'm also baking spiced apples and cherry pie. Isn't that right, my darling?"

I kiss my lover on his cheek.

*

The man, looking uncomfortable and tugging on the vest of his three-piece suit, nods and looks into my eyes that sparkle like the North Star.

"I wish you a Merry Christmas, miss." Walking away, he turns to look back, studying my sole figure staring fixedly into that window.

I place my fingertips on the glass and inhale deeply.

*

"Isn't that funny, dear? That man in the three-piece suit acted as if he didn't even see you.
He must be terribly lonely.

I, however, don't know what it is to be lonely,
for I have you, my love.
I have you,
after
we die,
and die,
and die again."

I look longingly at the display once more.

"Someday we shall sit around our own Christmas tree all gussied up with white lights, silver tinsel, and strings of popcorn made by our beautiful children."

What a wonderful life we'll have.

The snow falls charmingly.
I catch a flake on my tongue.

LOST FALL

Rainfall came late that year. Light lost in vortexes and spheres.

Was I gone too long?

    Left him behind, left him alone.

Season

    shifted

        to

            season.

                Ration could not find reason.

Moonbeams slid by, opening their opaque eyes. Each watched me closely,

ragged and

unlovely.

Once upon a time a pin-up girl... Harshest winds whirled and swirled around my nakedness.

I was suffocating but still held on to the pole tightly;

It was now too late to say goodnight.

Season   shifted   to   season.

      Ration could not find reason.

No diamond on my finger. Visions and scents of him lingered.

I've been gone much too long,

but I vowed to

    die

or find my way home.

Spring was around the corner, yet winter

would not turn over. Ox-eye daisies called, *"Come here!"*

I did not look back nor shed a tear.

      Season could not shift to season.

          Ration never found reason.

HAVE SOME CAKE

I whistle a tune that could irritate a saint, watching a couple hug and kiss endlessly. I think,
Why can't that be me? I killed the prom queen-
I thought that eliminated my competition.
A sad feeling comes into my heart.

I daydream of whore-red lips sipping a Bloody Mary out of a purple tinted glass.

I'm startled out of my daydream when a tall, beautiful, blonde-headed woman strolls by with a pink baby carriage and a ray of sunshine following her.
I ask God,
Why can't that be me?
A sad feeling comes into my heart.
I focus my attention on a handsome, very viral, dark-headed man. I undress him with my eyes and seduce him with my

smile until a tall, beautiful, dark-headed woman comes along, embracing my would-be hostage.

Damn! Out of luck again.

I say screw it, get a huge piece of German chocolate cake but only take small bites. A drunkard ambles past. I swallow one more small bite and offer him the remainder of this sinful delight.

He polishes it off, washing it down with the last bit of his pint. As he stumbles off, I yell after him, "Hey! Hey! You didn't save any for me!"
Damn! Out of luck again.
My mouth waters and my nostrils burn at the mere thought of the tasty brown stuff that killed my father. It is quite strange that I find myself asking God why he took my Daddy away from me.
A sad feeling comes into my heart.

I can't help but cry uncontrollably and am totally aware of the stares I am getting. I could care less. No one knows me anyway. I think God has forgotten my name.

Damn. Out of luck again.

I suppose I'll have some more cake.

ANIMAL KINGDOM

Lions in their lair.
    Stuck my hand in.
Shit. Caught in the snare.
    Body bare – abandoned.
Suddenly silent – enjoy the quiet.
    But note the venom everywhere.
Valleys so strange – arid plains.
    Rattlers scatter – coyly poised –
Here comes the noise.
    Their tails shake –
No poison to waste.
    Another life to take.
The lions appear – the chase is on.
    I'm outnumbered.
The snakes strike – the lions bite.
    Attacking front to back.
Fury unsurpassed.
    No place to hide.

Watchful eyes roll away on a dime.

    Contemptuous natures.

Brazen is the hunter.

    This is on you –

You stuck your hand in the lair.

    Body was bare.

You teased - they're pleased.

    The animal kingdom wins.

HOW DOES YOUR GARDEN GROW?

Family of three

in an old wooden house.

Father's feet creek

on the steps

while mother buries baby dolls

in the concrete next to the

garden.

Cardboard placards

of corn cobs and watch dogs stand

among the dandelions that overgrow.

Mother rakes the hoe.

Morality disposed of like

the weeds she pulls.

Can you see through this child's eyes

in the garden so corrupt?

Depraved behavior.

Tattoo of the little one's savior

on Father's arm.

Mother isn't alarmed

by the shameless affairs.

No restraint,

only degeneracy in the garden

behind the old wooden house.

Feet creek on the steps

while mother breaks the bough.

Little child never sleeps.

The fields need plowed.

DON'T FORGET THE WATER

I

Was the precious purity just a lie?

Family ties were in disguise.

The holiest of water streaks through the years.

Many voices echo, *"We love you, my dear."*

But they never led me to safety or

Freed me from their chain.

II

The holy water burns my skin.

Patience wearing thin.

The serpent slithers into my mind,

Whispering, "You're not His kind."

I'm tired. I'm hot. I need to be seen.

The battle rages, dirty against clean.

III

The whisper returns, "Come on, darlin,
Give me some fire. Don't be mean!"

Burn, baby, burn!
Ashes, dust, needs so dire.

Bunch of fucking liars.
Snake bites – I take flight.

IV

I'm getting hotter and hotter.
The wildfire surges.

Hell is around the corner.
Each one of my leaves is ablaze.

Flames rage and I remember
I forgot to bring the water.

BOOK II
KEEPING UP WITH THE JONESES

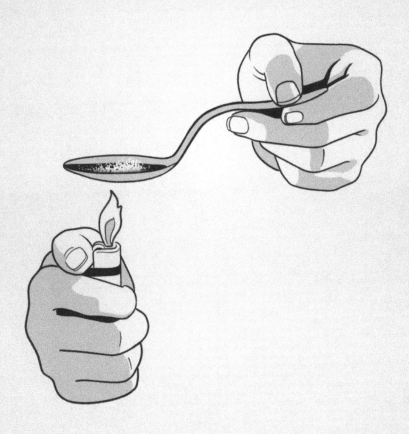

I DECLARE WAR

The battlefield is covered

With razor-sharp terrain-

Muddy rivers try to swallow me whole

I shove the rig in my vein/

Blood spits at me incessantly, relentlessly.

Forgotten days.

Confused about pain.

I succumb to the stain;

Abel is slain

PLASTERED DISASTER

whiskey whispers,

hey baby, did ya miss me?

tisk tisk

fuck this

bag of smack

so divine and sweet

dip that cig in pcp

please take me

crazy in the rain

out of this life

permanently insane

desperately proclaim

just say yes! i'm the best

i'll fuck you up

put you to the test

knocked you down

oops! dragged you back

damn that smack!

can't stop, can't care

won't stop, don't dare

here come the flies i so despise

never leave,

never give in

gritty sin

shovel the dirt

over my head

maybe this time

i'm finally dead

stuffed my head

with medication

indoctrination

new age meditation

vaccinations

just a vacation

--

finally been taken

crazy in the rain

gone from this life

permanently insane

THE LIST

Hands in hot water, scrubbing harder.

Virginal and pure, tainted no more.

Tight on my wrist pink roses sit, baby's breath rests.

How do I know I'm on the list?

It's humid, but I don't sweat.

Clean as the white moonlight.

The gnawing hits, persists.

The question creeps in – am I on the list?

But still, I wait, as cars pass by.

One, two, three - did he forget about me?

Petals begin to wilt, baby's breath is rank.

Shame washes over my heart as it sinks.

I shiver and hold myself

Despite the stifling air.

I will not tell her,

I would not dare.

I rip the strap from my wrist

And say, To hell with this.

Done sitting by the window,

Desperate to please.

I hit the pavement, running downtown,

Where no one will insist

I must be on the list.

Where I'm free to get my fix.

My hands are now dirty.

I roll up my sleeve

And cook up my date,

So beguiling and charming.

He won't make me wait –

He loves me without condition.

Spoons in hand, we hop and skip

Down the highway of perdition.

STARDUST

Garbage litters the strip.

Cigarettes burn their bottom lips.

Euphoric trance - take a sip.

One, three, six.

Choice is a head trip.

Incubus pulls out its horse whip.

It's just a chip, not a slip.

Lance slides into each pit.

Filthy dresses stripped.

Vulnerability unzipped.

The great white moon dips.

One, three, six.

Advance! Experience the drip.

Romance the same script.

No dues or fees for membership,

Only anguish to inflict.

All eyes closed on this mothership.

Awaiting the apocalypse,

Each junkie prays they won't get hit

With the one, three, triple sixxx.

RED WAGON

Floating in outer space, away I waste.

The stars scramble in haste.

I desperately, raggedly call out to you.

Where is my red wagon?

You sigh and reply,

I'm no longer so fucking blind.

I've guessed your secrets,

won't listen to your lies.

I cry. Please help me

        one more time

and pull me back to earth.

You eye me warily –

Alright.

        One more time.

Into my red wagon I climb.

Shaking and weak,

I collapse, so relieved.

I promise I won't fall out again.

  Trust me.

You do, harrowing as it is.

Pulling me around

gentle, yet strong.

Nourishing me.

  You trust me,

    praying you're not wrong.

Suddenly, the itch rushes over me,

the itch that must be scratched.

I oh-so-stealthily

climb out of my red wagon.

My secret is out.

No more lies.

I'm sorry. Please forgive me.

Thank you for believing in me.

  This time I know

    you're leaving me.

The bitter truth is in your eyes.

AN ODE TO STARGAZERS

Nights of glory, mornings of shoddy memory.

Afternoons behind curtains drawn.

Nighttime is lurking, no birds chirping.

Time for the illusion of my story.

I can't see the colorful light

in my eyes, can't hear the roar.

Just dying to score.

Shouting drowns out the silent scream within.

Salty, painful sweat pours. More roars.

I can barely wait to get off.

Thoughts start to race,

anguish twisting my face.

I want to see the sun come up.
The only glimmer of hope I get
is when I see the yellowish sky.
One more score and I'll be done.

No one knows I'm locked in –
they just see the star.
How have I made it this far?

Maybe I'll make it.
The grip holds tight.

           Almost   done.
                   Almost   there.

I can feel the prick of the needle stick.
One more time to kill the sorrow.

I promise you, brightest morn,
I'll get clean
tomorrow.

TIC TOC

i stare at the clock.

                                   tic toc tic toc

blinded by toxicity,
numbers out of sight.

                                   tic toc tic toc

dissonance.
wild and unruly,
i was a carefree child.
but innocence is long gone.

can't see the numbers but
i hear the click of the clock.

                                   tic toc tic toc

how could I have known
winter took all?
i fell so fast, so hard.

cannot rise, cannot fall.
cannot stand, cannot call.

eyes fly open.

a hand floats by,
light and beckoning.

YES! i'm done.
i think i'm reckoning.
no more destructing.
but I can't take my eyes
off of the clock.

                    tic toc tic toc

...for shame, junkie -

                        it's just a

                        head

                                    game...

hand now buried in spiders.

compulsions weaving

my desires.

i hear the rumble,

look away from the clock.

tearing down the stairs,

no more cares.

adrenaline rushing,

heart madly beating.

hand is fleeting.

cold, quick exchange.

keep the change.

i can't quit.

so fuck the tic. fuck the toc.

i'm stocked.

CAT AND MOUSE

Scurrying past the alleyway,

quiet as a mouse,

I look ahead.

Determined today to stay straight

on my new path with hope,

no longer dread.

Then appeared the cat -

my fragility was under attack.

He sprung upon me,

dragging me by

my tiny mouse hand

back to the trap house.

Cravings out of the gate.

Gather, taste, don't ever waste

the hot, spicy rock

from down the block.

Lungs yearning,

stomach churning,

I take the bait –

overpowered by a need

oh so great.

The cat gathers up all the mice,

passing out pipe after pipe.

We beg him, Please! Let us be!

But this cat never plays.

We rue the day

he pounced upon us

with his temptations

and subtle invitations.

Our words are choked

out of our throats

with the first blast.

Hit so hard, fear has passed.

To the cat, we're a joke.

He sits, fat and pleased,

grinning at last.

Trotting towards the alleyway,

he seeks another hungry mouse

to snatch up and bring back

to the trap house.

Heed the warnings

from the mice gone before –

run as fast as you can.

One hit and you're done.

The cat will have won.

Before you know it,

you've come undone –

the next run will have begun.

THE WHEEL

We are alone. Isolated.

The only two left in this fallen world

we so light-heartedly destroyed

on that seemingly insignificant night.

Exploring the land, minds...

Soft, softer, softest...

The instinct to kill, pure and heavenly.

I take in the puffy silver

as the monkey hangs from the spokes.

Long hair entwined.

Easy breathing,

despite the thick smoke enveloping us.

The wars of the world are over,

peace belonging to you only,

belonging to me only.

I scoff at your feelings of guilt,

for I am not ashamed.

Miss Josephine does her Irish jig

while the man in yellow plays his Dulcimer.

You lean in for a kiss, but I reject your advance.

I just placed another delectable tab on my tongue,

ready to dance my own jig.

The crickets announce the sunrise.

I've just begun to slide side to side

one more time.

Disappointed and dejected,

you pack up and head back

to the center of the universe.

I know you will not mention your confusion,

your objection.

You won't ask why

I choose to fly to never never land

with Peter Pan, forgetting that you live

in what is real.

Nonetheless, you wait for the trip to end.

You too are bound by the curse of never-never land.

SHOOT TO KILL

Destination remote,

far away in Mesopotamia.

We race down the silk road.

There is no competition

on this expedition.

No need to ask permission

to dive into a patch

of bewitching poppy plants.

Tropical yet temperate,

conditions so soothing.

We release all inhibition.

Remembrance of death?

That's just a superstition.

The Westerly wind flows.

Into this glorious patch we dive,

ignorant to the swine

forming a forceful line.
We roll around in the
sea of poppies,
tranquil and thrilled.

We suddenly see the swine
moving in for the kill.
Our screams are shrill -
"We haven't had our fill!"

Paul stands alone
in the distance
watching this debacle.
He shakes his head
at our insistence to
stay in this field of sin.

The swine wear us down
with attrition.
We say no prayers
of contrition.

Trapped in the patch,

the swine move in.

We surrender without will.

Going, going, going,

gone...

We become one

with the swine,

shooting to kill.

BLUE

In bed they crash,

in bed they dream

of a rewind, a redo.

Another shot

at something new.

Like a clean room,

a spring in bloom.

Maybe soon.

For now,

Jeanette and Drew

just fix.

They've tried to be smart

and change their ways,

but they've blown their chances.

The obsession won't fade.

Jeanette needs Drew,

the needle,

the spoon.

She sighs,

I can't live without any of you.

They are driven, drawn,

pulled into the undertow.

Drew holds on tightly

as they're dragged

into the black lagoon.

He never drops

their needles and spoons.

If he does,

they're surely through.

The shore of the lagoon looms,

but Jeanette and Drew

end up blue.

BOOK III
ALIEN-ATION

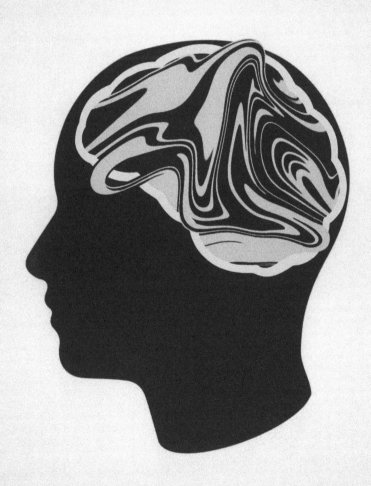

EXTRATERRESTRIAL BEINGS AND SUCH

Fractured from the human race/

The Alien Nation governs each of us/

Pumped full of Haldol and Prozac/

Behind locked doors/

--

Neurons misfire ----- like jammed shot guns/

Heads ache/

shock waves break/

--

Aliens cannot be people/

Life on earth is incomprehensible/

Just as extraterrestrial beings/

Look strange and distorted to you.

THE KING'S TABLE

Long, bountiful table,

the king seated at the head.

Dukes and earls, none quite able

to understand his queen,

who's not quite stable.

She violently jerks, laughing oddly,

calling for the jesters and clowns.

The king quickly angers

and commands the queen

to sit her ass down.

Shimmying onto the floor,

she crawls between the legs

of each duke and earl,

pissing off the king even more.

She makes her way to the foot

of his mighty chair

and dares him to take a swing.

The dinner guests are awkward and silent,

looking downward at the golden plates

that hold potatoes and meat.

The king sternly commands his queen

to take her goddam seat.

She rips the crown of pearls

from her hair piled high.

Fuck you! she shrieks.

I'm done with this life!

I just want to die!

She tears the corset from her chest.

The table collectively gasps.

Such behavior for a royal queen!

Exquisite one moment,

a ball of madness the very next.

The king apologizes for her mess,

muttering, she does this all the time.

The queen throws a crystal chalice
to the other side of the palace,
takes a chard and cuts her wrists.

Dinner continues to the 4th course.
Slash after slash the king ignores.

As he eats and entertains,
he pushes her cries aside.
He's seen her do such things
so many times,
but never believed
she'd actually succeed
in committing suicide.

THE EYEWALL

Pressure is low,

so insidious and sly.

Perplexities begins to rise.

My logic, my reason,

flee with the tide.

The storm is brewing,

the frenzy is mounting…

Circulation leading

to annihilation

with the power

of an atomic bomb.

Fragmented

                     is

     my

                             comprehension.

Thoughts ---- ideas---- notions ----

ripped to shreds

in one swift motion.

Thunder clashes,

lightning flashes.

Ring of clouds

all around.

Thrust into the surge,

my brain is

under siege.

Locked in this vault.

Is it my fault?

The high pressure

feels so good ----

my perception

shifts upward,

building heat and energy.

Peculiar and perverse,
the animal in my brain
needs fodder.

Raindrops pelt harder
with every darting thought ----
here, there, everywhere.

Fitful and fickle,
no circumspection.

I'm driven
into madness,
crazed and demented.

Stuck on green.
Every storm
is unseen.

The maniacal voices

long to rest,

to find the eye,

the clearer skies.

Yet the impulse drives.

My times in the eyewall

are insanely divine.

I don't want to

come down.

My body is screaming,

please break out!

Find your way

to the eye!

But I swirl in

wind ---- rotation ---- frenzy ----

Nothing can eradicate me

from this warm core.

The pain is so pleasurable,

I just want more.

MOURNING DOVE

I locked myself away

in a black wire bird cage.

Lost the key.

Couldn't break free.

I cringed and moaned.

Pain rippled through my brain

from everywhere and nowhere.

I'm not safe alone.

I can't crack this code.

Incarcerated behind the wire,

I settled in, terrified and mystified.

No locksmith for hire.

While I huddled in the corner,

an apparition descended,

extraordinary and watchful.

My name it endeared.
I asked this benevolent spirit,
what do you see?

It answered with no hesitancy,
I see a mourning dove
that's not sure it wants the key
to fly out of its cage
and get on its way.

I paused for a moment too long.
The kind spirit was gone.
I struggled to open my mouth,
desperately tried to open my eyes.
My throat and lids were paralyzed.
Find the key!
So much unsaid, unseen.

A malevolence descended upon me,
nailed me down in this jail.
Once again, I failed.
I can't post bail.

Screams were primal.

No more denial.

Put on trial, the verdict is final.

Guilty is the decision.

I am naked, one feather at a time

dropping on the cold floor

of my own prison.

Lost is my chance to fly.

BLOODLETTING

The taxicab speeds through long tunnels. 100, the speedometer reads.

I start to feel the dark matter, that dimension never mentioned. I tip the cab driver and say, "So long,"

entering the land of self-sovereignty.

No more theoreticals, no more if only's.

Each string suspended side by side,

we propagate.

No longer lonely, colossal energy pervades, multiplies, generates.

No need to persuade any of us to harvest with sickles and blades.

Hacking away at injustices with swipe after swipe -

one cut,

two cuts,

dripping red proliferates.

Razor flicks spark in the matter so dark. The victory brings much relief. No judgment at all, we're allowed to free fall.

Here in the dark, we relieve the pain,

the tension.

Each of us matters in this dark dimension.

SOLD

Ladies and gentlemen, behold!
Your story is about to be told...

They gingerly stepped on
the reddest of carpets,
donned in rubies and tarnished gold.

1,000, 2,000, 3000 – sold.
So many riches covered in mold.

Ladies and gentlemen,
dot the "i's" and cross the "t's"
on the line you sign
to never grow old.

Perceptions, projections.
Welcome to the cold.
Settle into this icy hole.

Ladies and gentlemen,

your story is the same.

Everything to lose, nothing to gain.

Ravaging coercion, radical conversions.

Brace yourself for essential pain.

It's always easier to blame the acid rain.

Ladies and gentlemen,

careworn and destroyed -

Open, terrific, threatening wounds

never to heal or ever to avoid.

Welcome to the special corner of hell

full of past lives.

Youth and age asunder,

but plenty of photos and toys.

How can you all now wonder

why you're conjuring up memories

of when you were girls and boys?

No more rubies, only injection blunders.

Now you'll never grow old.

1000, 2000, 3000, sold.

Damn good thing fans are faithful.

Your story has been told.

MOVING PICTURE

Riding the lightning,

so very frightening.

She can't stop screaming.

Shut up! Quit attention seeking!

Hot flood runs through

the tiny butterfly in her wrist.

All at once, warm and soothing.

The room is clearing.

Ready - set – convulse.

Check her pulse.

Charge, check once more.

She fell to the floor.

Seizing, sneezing, wheezing.

Frigid cold as a witch's tit.

A moving picture tumbles forth –

Here comes mother. Oh shit.

Slaps that cigarette

out of her hand.

"Change your clothes!

Fix your goddam hair!"

Her stomach churns,

body now warm.

Movie fades.

She's finally awake.

The reality of the starkest white.

Void of life, void of fight.

Maybe the picture was lying.

But why is she still crying?

BOOK IV
TOXICOLOGY

A VIRULENT STRAIN

Frag-ment/ary

remains, bitter and

despairing.   Tormented by

the proclivity to stay.

Weakness is   tender.

Surrender to lust.

Disambiguate love

and eros,

deconstruct   idolatry.

Claw at

the mistrust.

THE LAND OF NOD

You cup your hands,
>> bringing the sweetest nectar
>>> to my begging lips.

I drink from those hands
>> I've known for so long,
>>> fooled in familiarity.

Our needs are fulfilled,
>> thirsts are quenched
>>> while hearts wrench.

I love you, don't leave me.
>> We seethe in mutual hate.
>>> Desire is animalistic, innate.

I look deeply into your steadiness,
>> on the brink of insanity,
>>> as you eye me mockingly.

So strong and in command.

    Yes! Yes! Fill me up. I beg you!

        No! No! Leave me be. I hate you!

I strike your face.

    Get us out of this place!

        Your cheek is crimson.

Your wicked sight scathes me,

    plays with me,

        betrays me.

I crush my mouth to yours.

    You lament.

        Please don't leave.

Empty promises made,

    knowing they'll be held sacred.

        For you know, and I know,

We'd both cease to be

    without you holding me up,

        without me helping you breathe.

Bound together, we know we're forever.

    Lost in this land - we start over

        in agonizing terror and pleasure.

INVOCATION

Bells ring through the dusk, soft and low.

    Smokey eyes narrow.

    Sultry pout on her lips.

Wrapped in black lace and chiffon,

    she twirls in graceful circles.

Violin strums through the twilight, soft and low.

    Black-shaded eyes dart.

    Lips part ever so slightly.

Silver feathers cascade from her hair.

    Arms open to the onyx sky.

Witchy apparition

    that used to be a lady

    sways on.

Breezy is the eve. Song murmurs

    from the deep.

A man in a fedora with a smooth walking stick
    sees her through the looking glass.
    He reaches out to feel her.
Fingers slip through a reviled hallucination.
    She morphs into a silken raven.

A tambourine jingles in her hand, soft and low.
    Head bowed in supplication,
    he is besieged by an invulnerable force.
He refuses to abjure his hope that he can hold her.
    She gracefully twirls away.

A disintegrated mirage.
    Tear slides from his eye.
    The music painfully fades.
Blinded by his sorrow,
    he walks away from the glass, now stained.

EMMA

I see, smell, taste your loveliness. Love long ago
consummated with the gentlest caress.

I turned a blind eye as you plummeted from my sky.
Eden turned to Hades with one solar eclipse.

All I've known was the yellow and orange,
your body aglow.
When, oh when, did it turn to stone?

If only the stars hadn't decomposed.

Silent proclamation I refused to hear
throughout your descent into the sinkhole.

I grasped at the succulent, colorful fruit
now turned sour.
In the distance I heard the piano man
pounding on his keys, hour upon hour.

I wondered, waited, wandered.

Now the clock has run out. More time squandered.

I watch the finality of my Emma's demise.

I stepped away in manner and word.

Your spirit has been picked at, chipped at,

ravaged and wrecked.

So contrary to my beautiful woman

who used to glow in orange and yellow.

I almost succumbed to the invitation,

the temptation, the familiar sensation.

But I must bow out, exit stage left.

My heart is bereft with a sad remembrance

of my beautiful dreamer.

Emma, Emma,

I long for the paradise of Eden, but your remains

have disintegrated in your manufactured abyss.

DANCE, BALLERINA, DANCE

Rabbits, gnomes, and half-smiling trolls scattered when I entered their secret hiding place. As I laced up my slippers, the trolls knowingly snickered at the rabbits and gnomes who were afraid. A cool breeze blew lightly as an angel and a devil invited me to dance just this night.

The angel, iridescent and docile, on my right.
The devil on my left, on her lips a sensuous pout.
They both danced across my back.
I didn't have a way out.

No longer uncertain, a purple rabbit opened the curtain. I curtsied an invitation to these creatures of the night.
I twirled among the majestic trees, not sure which way to leap. Light chased dark as I floated through the air and landed on my feet.

As I continued to dance, I didn't even glance at the shirtless man who had been watching me all the while. The devil threw him a grin. The angel pressed, "Don't give in."

My eyes drifted in his direction. His couldn't quite meet mine. I was not inclined to invite him to dance but the devil wanted her time. I caved under the pressure, holding my hand out to this dark prince. My eyes then fixated on his muscular arms and chest.

I couldn't feel the angel on my shoulder wince. I was quickly lost in two black pools, seductive yet slightly bitter. Naive to this dark side, so easily fooled, I should have known better. If only I'd let the angel guide me instead of gliding across the ground in the arms of a man I'd never understand, only to be bound to for years to come.

The trolls grinned cunningly, for they could have told me how the story would end. But when I started to dance, I didn't have a chance to escape him and the devil's wiles. The rabbits and gnomes did not know I'd fall prey to the night and lose sight of the wise angel I'd left all alone. Now imprisoned in a prism, my dance is no longer my own.

DETONATED HEART

Hold me!

You shall not want for anything.

Concupiscent waves wash over me.

        Desperately wanting

        comfort in your strength,

        my heart steps on the battlefield.

Stay one more night,

stay within my reach.

Satisfy my voracious appetite.

        Desperately wanting a man

        who always eludes capture,

        I continue to refuse reality.

I will not cease fighting,

which greatly amuses you,

even in this rapture.

For there is no safety
in my imaginary world.
You warn me repeatedly,
run for cover, my delicate lover.

Desperately wanting
to shut out your words,
I cover your lips with mine.

You pull away, pack your bag,
brown, black and tattered.
Kiss my forehead with solicitude.
Whisper how much I mattered
on this celestial longitude.

But you must go
on the wings of the eagle,
place me on a shelf
(highly decorated)
and do what you can for your people.

PRAY FOR RAIN

Hours pass as freely as the storms come and go in the shithole called Middle America. We talk until our mouths are sandpaper. A quick caffeine
fix waters the Sahara as we talk for hours more. Yes! We debate. Discussions of what is literature and what is not. Are we born a clean slate?

Mother Change tries to drag us back to swing sets and hurt. Salty streams streak my cheeks while yours remain a block of concrete. I am frightened. "Don't look like that!" I chip away and get nowhere.
"A Republican will get elected," you say.
I shout! "Who gives a damn!"

You look at me pointedly and reply, "Why are you concerning yourself with what will never matter?
Democracy will still be anarchy in disguise."

You are calm, calculated. I am wild.

My eyes frantically search yours for something, anything. I can't see beyond the blue. The streams continue to flow as you move on, pouring meaningless words. Meaningless now, today, to me.

The white-hot fire in my soul has been put to rest by the hard, pelting rain. "How did I end up in this godforsaken part of the world?" You ask in return, "Why are you concerning yourself with what will never matter?"

VANISHING ACT

As I lie horizontal, my body spasms.
I'd trade my weight in gold for one more orgasm.

Hedonistic, not quite sadistic, wickedly wonderful.
Nothing ordinary or cheap. Weightless you come
to me before I sleep.

Your skin is translucent. My eyes, so hungry,
stare and stare.
Nothing's there.

I anxiously wait to open the gate of the fantasies you create.
I blink from my stare only to see
I'm left empty and bare.

Where is my phantom?
Naked and ashamed, I still lie horizontally
in this huge bed alone.

I'm saddened with riches, platinum, and

precious stones.

I try to pretend you never appeared here in my lonely space.

Then I remember, my anomalous, prodigious,

fantastic phantom -

I never even saw your face.

RED LEAVES IN MANHATTAN

A spider weaves its web on a leaf in Central Park

While a gentleman lay on his rooftop,

Blinded by moons.

Maybe she'll come. Maybe soon.

Visions of golden green come alive.

He fancies her so, the smiling Irish girl,

From the other side of this world.

Along came the spider, weaving a web on his heart.

Still alone, he wonders where she could be.

Into the park he looks but cannot see.

Hands on the clock tick and tock, the moons dark.

She dances through the delicate web and quietly slips away.
Sadness flows and ebbs.

Autumn in New York, save for a single leaf.

Green and gold fade away.

Aching, he cannot stay.

Falling brought freedom,

Freedom from his vanquished heart.

Eyes closed, gone is the final hour

And his web of woe.

ENDLESS LIVES

You rest with the sun,
coming alive, like a wild coyote,
with the beams of the moon.

Faster, faster, faster
goes the fire truck -
higher, higher, higher
you and I climb.

We are kites, invincible kites,
teasing and mocking the sky.
I open my arms
to the crushed diamonds.
You reach up and steal one
just for me.

I drop to my knees in worship of you,
ruler of our twisted little kingdom.
"Whatever would I do without you?"

you wonder, mystified.

"Die," I reply.

"But with me by your side

we have endless lives."

You accelerate – we spin out.

Nevermind the

skid

marks.

The blue pigs roll and grovel on demand.

The red and black ants follow you

in a neat, straight line.

The white puppets dance on command.

All your subjects, under your control.

You and I, in our cherry bomb,

explode in a rain of fire.

It's time for you to rule again.

Our souls seize in the pyre.

BOOK V
CASUALTIES OF EVE

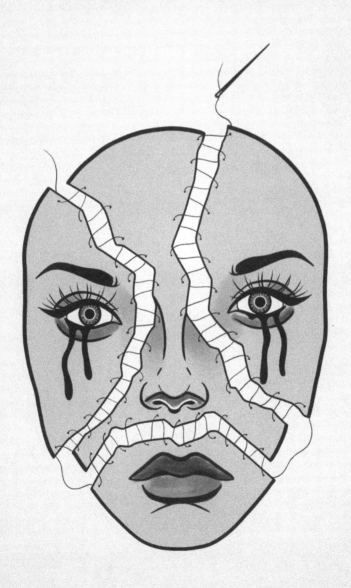

UNE FEMME TRISTE

swallow the jagged pill --

scorch

and

sear.

paralyzed

with anguish,

she   finally   combusts --

please let her rest.

wipe away the lifetime of tears.

MELISSA

Small and flaxen,

she drifted with vagabonds

across the borders, scarred.

Unsure.

In her lap sat

books of maps.

Barrage of words on pages

worn, ragged, torn.

From small to smaller,

numbers out of order,

letters skewed.

No marker of where

she was born.

Shattered chapters,
the cover a large factor
in how she learned
to smile on cue.

Passerby's never saw
beyond the fence.
Panic and static in the attic,
rats at war.

Turmoil exploding
behind enemy lines.
Broken bottles of wine
on the scoured floors.

Buried in her nest,
books in the treasure chest,
the wind shifted to the West.
She couldn't keep up the pace
and got lost in time and space.

Her life story reads

one short paragraph

in this epitaph:

> *"She was small and flaxen,*
> *lips curved in a bow,*
> *cover never blown.*
> *Here lies Melissa,*
> *lost on a map,*
> *origins unknown."*

GIRL GONE MAD

Platinum hair slicked back,

black eyeliner smeared.

I caught a glimpse

of

        a   fragment-ed

                    face

in the cracked rear-view mirror.

I stood on the shards of glass,

electric guitar in hand.

"Okay fans! Let's strike up the band!"

We sang a mad love song

to the girl who lived there,

where she played in the backyard

without a worry or care.

She lived her life like rock and roll.

Mother never approved.

Sex and drugs turned her out,

lascivious and lewd.

She ran away with that boy so bad.

I looked at this girl I saw far behind

                and asked,

                "When did you go mad?"

                She replied,

"Mother wanted me to marry

a nice man in a suit

who went to work, went to church,

and would make a good daddy.

I wonder if that one would have

made a good daddy even though

he was the unemployed atheist type.

I'm so sorry baby, please please forgive me.

I'm so sorry mother, please please set me free.

All I wanna do is dance naked in the rain

and sing off key.

'Cuz even though I can't sing,

I know I can dance enough to get by."

DADDIES AND DAUGHTERS

Daddy, Daddy,

I adored you so.

Once upon a time,

you were my hero.

Then you charged into

my pretty world

on your big red horse.

Hand heavy, breath hot

with the curse of our people.

Kisses soft on my sweet tears

after the fire.

Daddy, Daddy,

I loathe you so.

You are no longer my hero.

I've grown tired of this war

to settle the score.

Tired of your purple horse

that used to be red.

Nobody ever asked me, you know.

I'm all grown up,

you drunken fool.

Not the little girl you once knew.

I am my father's daughter,

nothing I wanted to be.

My temper runs deep

and ugly as yours.

Now, you bastard,

whatcha gonna do?

I am my father's daughter,
nothing I wanted to be.
What you said always mattered.
You made me a lamb for slaughter.

Daddy, I have yet to forget
your threats and the stank
of your cigarettes.

Daddy, I have yet to forget
your voice and your cutting tongue.

The razor continues to slice my eyes.
The scars are images I despise.
All of your lies have come true.

Daddy, I have yet to forget
everything I had to lose
as your begotten daughter,
the lamb for slaughter.

I cannot tell the false

from the true.

Double barreled shot gun blasts.

The curse is on me, too.

Daddy,

How can I forgive you?

FEARLESS

Zoe strutted down the streets of our quiet neighborhood

in neon miniskirts and purple fringed boots, getting away

with it.

She sat at my mother's kitchen table,

lit up a Camel Wide, then curtly told my family to go to hell

when asked to smoke outside.

She made my father chuckle under his breath,

gave my mother another reason to roll her eyes heavenward,

and had my little brother jerking off for weeks.

When my grandmother asked what her father did for a living,

she politely asked my 80-year-old granny to kiss her ass.

Zoe painted her face with glitter and green

because she didn't give a damn about anything.

The one thing she never did was open the door.

She remained silent when I told tales of
Barbie dolls, prom dates, and confirmation veils.

I watched in awe as she pulled a little mirror
out of her gold spangled purse
and snorted a line right there in the ladies' room.
I asked her if she was afraid. Her piercing laughter echoed in
my ears. She scoffed, "Fuck no! Fear is for losers who can't
get laid."

I adopted her philosophy and did my first line. I instantly
understood how easy it was to fly.

Then I saw the other side of fearless when she moved away.
My mother sighed with relief.

The neighbors talked for a while about that crazy girl with
the short skirts, all the men she took to bed, the sinful way of
life she led.

I stayed clean until Zoe was dead.

I lit up a Camel Wide with her Bic that emblazoned an engraved "Z", snorted an eightball,

and cried for my friend who couldn't.

A LETTER FROM SYLVIA

To my dearest,

Do you remember when I was pristine?

Poetry and prose written by a queen.

Desirous, salacious, untamed.

I did not know you had a name.

To my dearest,

Do you remember your secret invasion?

I needed no persuasion.

What was once a pleasant dance of one

Became an unsent letter and a loaded gun.

To my dearest,

Do you remember your fury and hostility?

How you denounced my femininity and fragility?

No relational planes of black or white

To your sarcasm and my strife.

Now, my dearest,

I am not free of your restraint.

All that was lovely has been slain.

Before the ink dries on this page

I will be six feet under your stifling rage.

BODY BETRAYED

…The pain of fame.

Amber remnants remain

of the voices that blame,

the voices that shame.

Deflowered in one snapshot.

An object to be used,

a burden to be carried.

A problem that cannot be solved.

Body betrayed, in the way.

Can no longer obey.

Used to be prime,

used to be elite.

Now lost in defeat.

Violation, suffocation
in Palisade Park.
Exhausted to the core.
But I'm the whore?

No more satin, no more lace.
No lust in my eyes
or smile on my face.
What a surprise.

Antithetical to the famous,
contrary to the rich.
Snap! Snap!
What a bitch.

Body betrayed, in the way,
refusing to obey,
amber remnants remain.
I will not stay
for this rapid decay.

Body betrayed, in the way,

no longer able to obey.

I will not stay.

Amber remnants fade…

MY NAME IS LISETTE!

The theater, the theater.
Oh, the drama of the theater!

Daffodils line the stage.
Wild dogs salivate.

The audience anticipates
the performance of a lifetime,
shocking and fantastic,
with plenty of filth and grime.

Each seat is stuffed
with pink paper dolls
and fierce white tigers.
They drip in tanzanite
for opening night.
I burst out from behind
the ratty burgundy curtains.

"I am an actrice! My name is Lisette!"

I hurl black opals
into the wishing well.
The echo of the jewels
is loud as hell.

My screeching voice carries
as I open the first act.
Cut-out eyes drip black, contrite.
Blood spurts from the tigers' ears
under the pale lights.

Candy for my nose, script after script.
I get high on the lines that I snort and spit.
This play, such an event, so extravagant.

"I am an actrice! My name is Lisette! You came to be shocked, seduced, to feel freedom and fright."

I sing, I dance, I primp, I prance,

to show you impurity,

to rock your security,

to satisfy your secret fantasy.

"Any audience participation? Come, feel the degradation, so radiant and trashy! I'll hedge my bets no one's got the guts to be an actrice like me, so deviant and bizarre!

Believe me, cowards and thieves, bastards who always leave -look no further for the hottest fervor. My play goes on forever.

My name is Lisette. I aim not to please. As you sit on your asses, silent as can be, I will bring every one of you down to your knees. You will regret not betting on fame that's free. This actrice will visit you in every dream, a reminder of your faint-heartedness, spinelessness, and sleaze."

PRETTY

Mama, Mama,
      you were so pretty.
So pretty and
      so cold.
I loved you
      more
than any little girl could.
Had so many
      fan-ta-sies
that I would be
      pretty.
Didn't care that
      you never cooked
or practiced
      for my spell-ing bee
so long as I was
pretty
      and you would
notice me.

>>Then I wouldn't be so

>>lone-ly.

Mama, Mama,

>>You were so far away

>>in the house of cards…

>>I tried hard

not to breathe

>>so you would see

I was good

and pretty.

DID YOU KNOW?

Girl becomes fish,

fish on the shore of raging sea,

gasping for breath,

as they smother her face with a pillow.

Girl becomes kaleidoscope,

an array of radiant reds – blues - yellows

as they   kick/   slap/

      punch her/

Girl becomes channel,   outlet,

      point scored,

for their darkness/   their hate/

their animal rage/   their games -

Girl screams. No!

They laugh. Yes!

Then   all at once

      girl is no longer girl.

She is old, old woman

wondering where she went wrong.

Where the air -   the blood -

              the white went.

Where Mary went.

But oh, there, there! Boys will be boys.

She will piece together the remains,

mourn the loss,

dress in baggy clothes for no apparent reason.

Valium for sleep

and southern for comfort

while they go on the road more traveled,

        on probation, of course.

              Minus $500 in their pockets.

This old woman says, FRY THE FUCKERS!

Don't you know what no means?

As they search for another to steal the   breath/

      life--   love/ from

they chuckle.

Hell yeah, we know!

No means yes.

Didn't you know?

A DECLINATION OF GRACE

Three monarchs suffocate in a mason jar while
emeralds are lined with midnight's ink. Lips
are magnetic, bubblegum pink.
Sleazy glam stains the sink as the
butterflies gasp and mother weeps.
Graveyard tombs. I was not safe in her womb.
Obscene and unclean… Fists fly.
Mic drops. Cloudy is the sky. Steel city
cries - what a pity. quarters and dimes. one high
crime too many. The monarchs sigh, resigned.
Morals misaligned. Isn't she pretty?
A life, such a waste, shoved in her face. Declination
of Grace. Strobe lights flicker as she trudges
the path that is least traveled in a day.
Swallow the pill so jagged. She surrenders, a weak-
willed freak. Sledgehammer smashes the mason
jar. woke her/choked her/fought the battles,
lost the war.

Nothing left but scorn.

Crossbow pierces her words. "Quiet now, this won't hurt."

Ring around the Rosie. head in hands.

magpies fly. Each monarch dies.

Inky lined emeralds, bubblegum pink lips. She trudges the path least traveled each day and blows a final kiss.

BOOK VI
THE UNFORTUNATE SONS OF CAIN

WRATH

Advance. Invade. Denunciate.

My blood pumps furiously.

Father. Father.

Must I fight for your soul? Must I pay for your sins?

Thunder rumbles, commanding me

To march onward.

No room on this battleship

For sissies and cowards.

MAN ALONE

Big, angry hands

have felt damp thighs after sex,

moist ground after rain.

      These hands, my hands,

so quick to hurt,

yet seeking to soften, stroke,

ease their pain.

Feet, blistered and bruised,

have run from the light,

the blinding white light.

      These feet, my feet,

time to rest, to be washed,

cleansed, and renewed.

Memories, red and raw,

fade with time.

Honoring the code crossed the line.

      Visions in the back of my mind

find no ration nor rhyme.

Slanted, furious eyes, my eyes,

have seen green ink, golden tongues,

an array of blacks and silvers.

    They have bled in awakening

and cried.

Yet I am never satisfied.

HIS LOVERS

A Navy SEAL, highly decorated,

only known now

as a belligerent civilian.

The killer in him boasts,

"They never broke me."

Sprawled out on brown velour

that looks clean in the dark,

he observes his hands.

The right one is

clutching the remote

that tugs him into

a drunken sailor's fantasy.

The left one is caressing

that bottle that drowns him

in the good times of 1962.

The screen is the sea,

the bottle the erotic

dark-skinned lover

he had on a Pacific Island.

"WHY DON'T YOU LOVE ME?"

Eyes out of focus, he mumbles,

"You know how I love Jim Beam.

Now get me another bottle."

DAVID AND GOLIATH

Your story is scripted in black and

shades of gray. In an iron and steel cage,

you prepare for the fight today.

Expectant onlookers, frothing mouths galore,

scream for the carnage, the spears, the blood

on the dirt floor.

David, my love, so strong, so confused.

I alone know the truth of the lion on your chest,

the coat of arms on your back.

I alone know of the secret attacks.

You cannot rest because the world has

never seen you fail. I alone know your

dark spirit, fragile and frail.

Black, brown, and green created a killing machine.

So many Goliaths you slew. I alone know the only Goliath remaining is the one that lies within you.

No iron or steel can halt the great reveal.

Nonetheless, the crowd awaits…

expectations, anticipation.

Sweat pouring, hope soaring, you face a Goliath you've never faced before.

You raise your fists, take your stance.

More roars and cheers as you cleverly

escape the lingering mirror.

The audience is ready, the stakes are high.

Striations ripple from your arms and thighs.

You must look this Goliath in the eye.

Slay the one that haunts you, taunts you,

fills your mind with lies.

My beloved David, the time has come to walk away from the arena and find your way home.

The frenzied crowd dies down, filing out,

frown after frown, for they can't witness

the decisive battle.

It's you versus you, no Goliath in sight.

It's you versus you, right now, tonight.

Fight, my love. Slay the last Goliath.

Step into the light.

Slay him.

Come to life.

MUSE

Face and neck fire red, blue eyes, bulging.
Voice gravelly, veins popping. Skinny plaid tie,
holes in his shoes. Is he old news?

He collapses sharply on the concrete ground.
Unbeknownst to him, no longer renowned.
Romantic delusions entertained. He whispers
to a girl so stunning, "I'm not dead, just sleeping."

The rage was left behind on the stage. He hums
a melancholy melody, strums an imaginary guitar.
Stardom over too soon. Pause –
taste the metal spoon.

All he's seen and known; he still has no home. Romantic
delusions. It was all a lie that he refuted.
One thought too many, the very next hindered.
Love affairs vary. Is she kindred?

He fancies her, this stunning girl. A romantic
delusion's preview. She knew better than
to allow him close after he read the reviews.

Eyes now swollen and faded blue, blind to the truth.
He saw himself only in his youth.
Downgraded from star haze, he has no shame.
He revels in false fame.

Romantic delusions of a man once desired, he gave away his
good name. Now he cannot upgrade,
only be upstaged.

Life in ruin, but he does not know. He fancies her, this girl
so stunning. He takes off after her running at full speed,
humming a melancholy melody.

A PENITENT

Such invaluable loves in my cowardly world -

my could have been, should have been,

would have been… Cheyenne, Charmaine,

and Abigail.

I didn't pay attention to the pain I caused

as I left the first, second, finally, the last.

I couldn't see through my own greedy needs

to acknowledge I made your hearts break and bleed.

All of your love, so abundant; my actions, redundant.
Prelude to your hope I crushed with every step. I walked
away unscrupulously, thoughtlessly, as you wept.

Today, I rock in my chair and reflect.

What could have, should have, would have been,

if only I had behaved. I don't bother trying to forget. I
deserve this grief. I can't go back.

"I'm sorry" are such empty words. I wish I could make amends to my Cheyenne, my Charmaine,

my Abigail.

I place no blame on any of you

for refusing to let your hearts

bleed again.

I welcome the shame

and embrace the blame.

20 TO LIFE

The gavel slammed -

BANG.
20 to life.

Chance of parole in 15…
Fuck me man.
This wasn't in the plan.

Now here I sit, sink, a sort-of bed,
silver bowl to take a shit.

Had to get in the game to make it.
I scanned the yard searching out my kind -
otherwise, I'm left behind, open wide.
Nothing on my hands but time.

My pop died when I was a kid.
Set off my defiance, lit up my aggression.

Running the streets, my mum couldn't control me through threats or beatings.
My rage couldn't be contained.
We were good. Roof, money, food.

Then BANG.

My Pop got shot by some jagoff over a parking spot.

Next thing I knew I was hanging in the empty lots, drinking, plotting, smoking, scheming.
I always saw RED.

Dude looked at me sideways.
RED.
Some broad dissed me.
RED.
My mother yelled at me.
RED.

You'll end up dead!
She begged. She pled.

Then I stuck a needle in my arm and bled.
Fuck. I missed. So I tried again.

BANG

I shot up like a champ.
The dope turned the
RED
to light blue.
Then I knew I could make it through.

The robbing started.
The stealing, wheeling, and dealing.
Bottom line - I needed the green to score.

Held up a drugstore, desperate and sick.
Old lady tried to call 911,
so I stabbed her in the neck.
Busted anyway.

I kicked in county.
Thought I was going to die.

Shitting, puking, freezing, shaking.

I took a chance at trial.

Thanks to my dumbass lawyer

it was over before it began.

BANG

20 to Life.

I got my crew here. Do what I have to do.

Try to keep cool. No more

RED

blinding my sight.

Just duct tape gray and white.

I'd shake the out hell out of that 12-year-old boy,

but there's no turning back.

Got to do my bid. Try not to kill or die.

My mum gets me by. She visits and writes.

Says she prays a rosary for me every night.

Not sure how Jesus feels about me, but I'll take it.

I do not blame my Pop's death for this cage.

Done are those days. I did this to myself.

I look forward to the time in the yard.

Hoping I don't get shanked, I keep my eyes blank.

Trust no one. Just enjoy the hours of sun.

ANIMATION FASCINATION

Red spikes in his skull,
bony body contorting.

The bullet train barrels
toward the railroad crossing.

Warning! Warning!
Step away from the tracks!

Shiny black latex clings to the
woman cranking the phonograph.

The rolling rock, aces,
and bass come to life.

Drums beat in strife.
Cards are dealt.

Blackjack table packed.
Will he play his hand or fold?

Beware! Beware!
Screams climax.

Blood-stained fingers
strike the bass.

Faltering, to their chagrin.
Bullet train on its rampage.

The women scatter.
The drums beat louder.

Fascinated by the animation,
pretending to surrender.

Admissions, confessions.
All lies told at the railroad crossing.

The wrong way he went.

The partygoers were spent.

Come back! Come back!

The bass groans.

He throws down his cards.

with no deliberation -

Jumps on the tracks,

dismissing potential salvation.

GREAT SCOTT

Trash talking. Keep walking
away from the specter thrashing,
slashing my war-torn tome.
Short circuiting, melting down
in Tinseltown.

The more I seek
the louder they speak
in riddles and tongues.
Angst woven through my lyrics
unsung.

Agony here, there,
from everywhere and nowhere.
A nomad in the night, a note I write.

Apology necessary after

I'm buried in an idol's cemetery.

Shadows of dramaturgy

slip through the headstones.

I'm never alone.

Haunted by song and prose,

my final show never exposed.

The graveyard pulsates.

Don't be fooled.

My soul is not in repose.

HOME FOR THE HOLIDAYS

Chestnuts are burning on an open fire; Jack Frost is biting off my nose. Oh! What a happy time the holiday season is. A time to celebrate, eat, be merry (I suppose).

I'm not going home for the holidays this year.
There is no 8-foot-high Christmas tree with twinkling lights and candy canes. No gathering around the warm, cozy fire to burn the goddam chestnuts over or flickering candles on the windowpanes.

All that's left of home is a bitter, terribly old young woman who loves birds only and eats apples, lonely. How many times I've longed for her.
But fuck it.
I am left in the bitter cold to celebrate Christmas with my good friend Jack (that's Daniels, not Frost). I spar with him in the snow. I fall to my knees and pray to the

Virgin Mary, wishing I had some Cuervo, 'cuz it would mix better with the salt of my tears.

I stagger down the empty streets the night before Christmas, eyes wild as my dirty hair.
I clutch my black leather to me as I shiver and
what do you know!
I spot Father Patrick walking out the back door
of Our Lady of Angels. I thought him surely dead by now. I drag myself over to him and inquire,
Where is your Bud?

I mean, we're talking about a priest who always had a beer in his hand outside of the one mass he gave on Sunday mornings. He looks at my wild eyes and hair and gravely replies,
"Bud was not my friend, my child."

I roll my eyes and reach for the flask safely tucked in my boot. My eyes roll back around to meet his that aren't twinkling anymore. "Hey! Hey!

What happened to my favorite priest

who used to sneak me extra communion wine?"

He presses his rosary in my purplish-blue hand

whispering, "Please go home for the holidays."

My mouth flies open and I shout! "Fuck you then, old man!

I don't need you anyway!

You don't know anyway!"

I stagger on as the wind blows hard. My cold bones scream

out in pain.

Someday soon we all will be together... I curl up on a bench

with a raggedy orphaned cat and fall asleep thinking of my

mother.

I'm tired... So very tired... I sleep... I dream... I see a soft

white light, hear the lusty cry of a newborn baby...

A gentle hand clasps my shoulder,

guiding me to the final gates of home.

EPILOGUE

COFFEE BREAK

The air hangs thick, and my coffee is bitter and cold. I say
screw the coffee and fire up a Salem Ultra-Light 100 with the
yellow lighter my dream lover gave to me the night before, after
we made love on the dance floor in a hole-in-the-wall club
with psychedelic lights, men and women in ecstasy,
and me, caught up in the sweaty mix so I could feel like I
belonged just a little.

I take a long, hard drag off this poor excuse for a cigarette,
longing for a Lucky Strike, as I ponder
this freak show of existence I'm observing.

Suddenly, a handsome man sporting a 3,000-dollar suit and a
flashing gold band on his left ring finger
strides past me, giving me a suggestive wink.
In return, I give him my best Drop Dead, Bastard, Go Home
to Your Wife stare...

All at once my attention is diverted to a hard looking woman with witchy died black hair and pounds of pancake makeup on her worn face.

She is in the ring of fire, surrounded by a pascal of screaming children with noses running and diapers sagging. As I watch, one of the little girls is misfortunate enough to scream a little too loud so wham! goes the woman's hand with stuffed sausages for fingers across her offspring's pale little face. I roll my eyes in disgust and give this mother my best Great Parenting stare...

I tire of that part of the show and swivel around in my chair, listening to the cheap orange plastic crackle beneath me. Just as I vow to go back on a diet, an older couple sits down within earshot. The bald, overweight, loudmouth husband goes to get he and his wife two cups of the nasty sludge I had long ago abandoned. She offers to help him, but he informs her that he is quite capable of carrying two goddam cups of coffee. She shuts up instantly. I decide I hate them equally- him for treating her like shit and her for taking it. I give him my best

Just Who the Hell Do You Think You Are stare and her my favorite I Know a Good Therapist stare...

I wrinkle my nose, grind out my Salem, say screw trying to cut back and lighten up and quit. I head off in search of a pack of Lucky Strikes, hearing my mother's voice somewhere in the distance preaching the horrors of cigarettes. I find a newsstand and ask for a pack of my much sought after Luckies, paying a miserable looking teenager. I give him my all-knowing Just Wait Kid, Life Sucks More Than You Can Imagine stare...

Joyfully, gleefully lighting up a Lucky, I spot a scruffy but not dirty man perched on a step fondling a bottle of Coors. For some strange, maybe gravitational reason I stop short and look into his blue eyes twinkling beneath bushy brows of salt and pepper. Instantly- momentarily - we are connected, for he enjoys the show just as much as I do. He curses, laughs at, and cries for the actors too. He is reading my mind and seeing through my façade. He holds up his bottle to toast me because he knows I drink like a sailor and had only seconds before been judging him for drinking in the middle of the afternoon. I see all of this in his wise eyes so rather than silently curse him I smile knowingly and give him my best You and Me, We're of the Same Kind look... He nods and takes a long swallow of beer.

I think long and hard about that man and marvel over his insight- both of us drunks and both of us hypocrites. I laugh out loud at the irony of it all.

When I reflect on the man in his fancy suit and wedding ring, my mother's sermons on the evils of smoking, and that crabby bastard who was yelling at his wife for the 40th year in a row, I find it all downright hilarious, laughing uncontrollably.

Now I'm getting the stares, which makes me laugh even harder, so I give them all my Yes, I Just Flew Over the Cuckoo's Nest stare right back...

As I thoughtfully puff on my cigarette, I wonder who will be in the next act of the show, where I'll ever find a decent cup of coffee, and how many beers my new friend on the step has had by now. I sigh contentedly. A crowd bustles past hurriedly, heads down to avoid eye contact. I shout at the top of my lungs,

My friends!

When you do not look,

you fail to see

that every act of life's freak show

stars you and me…